UNCUT UNCENSORED
UNCENSORED UNCUT

BY

VERLENA SEXTON-WALKER

ISBN: 1-4140-2207-7 (e-book)
ISBN: 1-4140-2206-9 (Paperback)

Library of Congress Control Number: 2003097974

This book is printed on acid free paper.

Printed in the United States of America
Bloomington, IN

1stBooks - rev. 10/27/03

"In all there is insight in which given thoroughly can be a bigger investment in life than stock that has accelerated in cost and brought profit to your portfolio."

"In meaning, knowledge is sometimes more valuable than foresight…"

Verlena Sexton-Walker

06-20-2003

TABLE OF CONTENTS

<u>HUMANITY</u>

Why me

Why me

Is it the color of my eyes

The way I smile

Laughter you hear

To near

Question to ask

When you sense jealousy

That develops a false humanity

Why not you

You laugh to

Your smile shines

All the time

Answers to give

When people are not 'for' real

Creating self-preservation

And longer years

Why anyone

That has begun

To enjoy life

Beauty is seen

A process of the well-being

In which all is known

Through the perspective of love

That has grown

Why not laugh

As well as smile

IN THE MEANWHILE…

All will forever flow

An eternal glow…

"Happiness is for everyone why shun when you are not the only one [that should be happy]." (Verlena Sexton-Walker)

<u>CATASTROPHIC</u>

As I focus on what I know

There is a belief that unfolds

Of mankind in a struggle of captivity

No longer a belief or make believe

A process is diagnosis

This must be why they fuss

Because one will not accept authority

Of the guidance in a wrongful deed

As the vision is foreseen

The mission is place in destiny

With the sound of a jar in mouth

The noise ricochets through the house

A procedure is done

With a razor blade and a gun

Opening a wound so deep

Incision done while asleep

Lies are told continuously

"Maybe this will cripple," is said

While a bullet goes in the head

A catalyst of a thunderstorm

When the wounded is unharmed

Telling whom is hated as well as despise

Forgetting to know why

A focus, a vision, a mission

Improbable cause

This is just a concept after all

Catastrophic is displayed as a hole in a wall

<u>MISTAKEN IDENITY {FOOTBALL}</u>

The boy is in the room

Standing at the door holding a broom

Saying, "I am not a bitch but a male witch ready to snitch."

Electricity is my game

That will give me fame

As I interrogate you to point the finger at whom to blame

A head leaps out a fan

An image of a man

Commenting, "I had you."

In which he knows this is not true

Bouncing a basketball in a room not a hall

His eyes changes

Putting one leg forward

With pantyhose on

He yells, "Verlena I have won."

Leaping a head out of the fan

Is this an image of a man

Stating, "This was not plan."

While trying to shake my hand

What is his name

Vincent I believe

Misconstrued as well as malconceived

{MISTAKEN IDENITY}

<u>FACE-UP</u>

Despicable, loathsome, appalling

This is not a calling

To heal humanity of what they call wicked

A motor vehicle accident

Well not solve the problem

If there is something to despise

It comes through in false hopes and lies

Making eyes wild

As we here laughter of a child

In a cubicle all along

Humming, "The Thrill Is Gone"

Repugnant, vile, abhorrent

Surroundings in an environment

Of distasteful 'immigrants'

And ignorant idiots

Loath the man whom is always in black

Changing his eyes base on the attack

To give not a hint or a clue

Believe he can misconstrue

Hideous, gross, awful

Is the outside

The hair you chew on a rubber band

While you smile

Appall whom for what

Eyes protrude

Jumping in place

Take my time set the pace

Is what the man says

As he transcend through a wall

Over 'my' bed

<u>NO DREAM DENIED</u>

A pledge to American children

No dream denied

In a substance of neglect

A morality trail

To teach how to learn the best way for 'you'

Is a depiction of potential in what learning can do

The journey in life is 'never-ending'

In which there is always a beginning

To start at the point we left off

Not associating this to what it may cost

"No dream denied"

Should be a chant

Of hope for a better tomorrow

Disarming I can't

This excursion should be done by oneself

No one to follow your concept

Instead, develop it secretly

This is how you will succeed

Sharing once everything is in place

Amazing 'without' the grace

A MATTER-OF-FACT

Everything I do

Suppose to hurt you

I do it intentionally

"Do you believe me?"

Are those tears in your eyes

Why do you cry

You getting enjoyment out of this

As you deem and see fit

You ask, "Do I play?"

Listen to what I say

Purposely spoken

You think I am joking

Are you in grief

Or is that a sign of relief

Only false hope and a belief

FINALLY

Once the tone is set

The voice is pinched

Ready and able to call you a 'bitch'

SCARE AND SCAR {LAWLESS SOCIETY}

A female cop standing in streets

Spitting and talking while biting her lips and gritting her teeth

Cuffs a drunk

Throws him in the police car

Turns around yelling, "Motherfuckers go into that bar"

You a badge bitch

Full of bull shit

Play somebody else with your badness

Male cop breaking up a drug ring

Is a depicting scene

Says to innocent man

"Motherfucker I'll come back at you latter - You part of this plan"

The badge must be in your dick

Nothing but shit

Would a female fuck this

Or is male your preference

All 'white' male police precinct

Tells the 'niggers' you skink

While the black man writes 'murder ink'

To find out how these white men really thinks

Damn fool, you being mentally use

That's just a badge

Try sticking it up your ass

And than, maybe, you will be able to pass [gas]

All polices are 'just' a badge now

Do you ask yourself how

Because of racism, corruption, and injustice

This is what a preacher should preach

When they lack the ability to teach

You are a badge bitch

Nothing to help this

Enforcement of the law

Is just a pretense

Scare and Scar is evidence

"So many American cops are murder everyday. Statistics says this is the right way when injustice overrides justice, but who tallies the stats the police or civilians." (Verlena Sexton-Walker)

EASY COMES—EASY GOES

I am the one they say will pay

As I set the stage for the next prey

I think of what techniques to use

Trying not to confuse

The hub of life is prognosis

Making sure not to miss a dose

As the hope becomes the scope

Evangelizing injustice

And a practice of pretense

A visionary error that really does not make sense

Do you figure I care

Of whom you favor and what they wear

Believing you are everything

Ugly is what's under sunscreen

The focal point breaks all

As they believe they are winning

Be an ass all your life

Maybe someday you can think twice

And develop a new beginning

My bosom is so large

Says Patti

As she makes an ugly face

Is this a concept or what she calls grace

The centerpiece stands in the middle of the table

Balance it if you are able

To sacrifice your face

Or to put shame in its place

"In all is well," says the lady

Stirring gravy in a bowl

As the day changes to night

She becomes old

The concentration has ended

On an happy note

No one has to pay

A message delivered today

Push in my tote

As I walked away

LIFE CHOICES {REMEDY}

Bold, Italic, Capitalize

On a serious note

Of what you mean and what you wrote

Reading between the lines

Is not always easy

In all events, you will become sneaky and sleazy

What is that writing on the wall

Does it tells everything to y'all

Or is it a mistake that is being played

Reading is knowing what is meant

Regardless of the hint

Making sure time is well spent

When a message is received

Magical things can be seen

Of whom can make a difference

And what makes no difference

Indifference

Life choices

"Knowledge is given to those who wish to receive it and retain it. In all, you learn to know and you know to learn (wisdom)…KNOWLEDE BRINGS

VERLENA SEXTON-WALKER

ABOUT WISDOM AS WISDOM BRINGS ABOUT KNOWLEDGE..."
(Verlena Sexton-Walker)

<u>BLACKMARKET</u>

The side of my TV is disease

As I pick up my keys

Witnessing the final plan

The potency of the woman

Taking a stand

Am I afraid

Of course not

Crying, sucking in snot

This man is not real

Just an ugly bastard ready to kill

The timing chain goes rattle, rattle, rattle

As I hear the herd of cattle

Moving hyperactively

Fast pace without destiny

Monkey-like I am

As I depict this scam

Of whom she says she is

Utilizing Will

To use the blood in my veins

Is this another form of fame

Rattle, rattle, rattle goes the timing chain

Cattle, cattle, cattle is the game

Of the man that has no name

Kids—children all the same

Whom will take the blame

Than that 'woman' says be shame

"In life, there are many mistakes in which the biggest one of all could be the ones that God chosen to give us life—our parents (mother and father)…
The question remains to be, "Can mankind change God destiny in the life he gave 'me' and whom this life derived from?" (Verlena Sexton-Walker)

MOTHER TO THY MOTHER

FATHER TO THY FATHER

WHEN GOD CHOSE ME FOR YOU

WHY DID HE BOTHER

"Give all glory to the ones that deserve it in which it could be oneself."
(Verlena Sexton-Walker)

<u>PROFITEERED</u>

Professional athletic I am not

But I know when to take a shot

To argue with ignorant fools

Can be so uncool

When hippies is all you got

The disease of knowing what to say is in the mind

Continuous access can be a waste of your time

In the right mood, all you have to do is unwind

Sporting good store I stand in

Talking to a man about fish pins

As he begins to talk in slang

I knew I was ahead of the game

Is it truly a disease to know what to say and when to say it

Is this truly amazing

Pacing can make you crazy

Nerdy vs. promptness

Is ridiculous

Trying to change persona

Why would you wanna

Jealousy

Does not mean a damn thing to me

<u>MEDITATION</u>

Names of people that are at odds
Can make life tiresome and hard
When there are no ends to means
As you contemplate there scheme

I am not your enemy
She is
I am not your friend
He sees
That any relationship is impossible
As well as improbable

"Get it," says the boy outside
Get what and why
Are you worried about your trials
As you sharpen the hoe with the file

Who wishes that you would die
I am not your brother, 'the spy'
To say that you are tired of living
Is what life has given

Not all is love

Not all is hate

As we feed a famine

With what love takes

A WHITED PATHWAY

Mikki Moore is the name

As he begin to dream

That he is the splitting image of King

Saying, "Let freedom ring"

Civil Rights Movement was for blacks

Whom was constantly subject to the white man attack

Not to the telephone people

Nor the water man

Those are the people whom shake your hands

Pathetic Prothetic are the words use

When the people of color are confused

That the white man only scar and abuse

Never the ones they chose

The March on Washington was in statement

Of hate of racism

But all chose to walk that day

Did they pray

That this movement would never be repeated

Looking over my shoulder, they are misleaded

If you where born during that time

Something happen in the mind

Because of all the worlds, you seem to have created

Overlooking whom is truly hated

A riot took place in Detroit as an aftermath

Fooling the Negroes about that

The Civil Rights Movement being truly over

As the little black girl walked in the fields picking four leaf clovers

If you have a dream let it be known

Do not hold onto the torn

Putting all bad things behind you

This is what you need to do

Pray that your ideal is a concept

As you hunt for help

In what you love and hate

This is how Dr. Martin Luther King, Jr. became great

"When making chooses, be ahead of your game. Do not give the white man the black man fame when you are not appropriately aimed—oppression cannot be the blame, but, only the Negro shame." (Verlena Sexton-Walker)

<u>WHIRLPOOLS WHIRLWINDS</u>

Disintegrate, Ignite, Explode

Let go of that heavy load

Call hate

Because it's in your face

Making you out to be a disgrace

Waste of your time, Not mine

I look back, Not behind

This is an assumption of a man

That has a plan

To make me pay

In the end

Magnify, Cry, Why not try

To accomplish a vision

A finally

No indecision

Reality

A woman presumption

Is an accomplishment

Of what needs to be done

When none has won

Celebrate, rejoice, it's your choice

Opinion voiced

In detail of what is known

Expression shown

A child laughter

Heard afar

Is music to the ears

That can bring tears

Jump, pace, not in place

A clown face

Is the illustration of a poem

Imagination formed

CONSTELLTATION

The splitting image of King
Depicts what he will dream
As he walks on a stage
Singing, "Lift Every Voice and Sing"

The war is in the mind
Walking with arms crossed behind
Back against a wall
The scholarly fall

A little girl in the cornfield
Saw her father kill
By white man up the road
As she grows older
She tells her story

Fighting with yourself
Is not a sound concept
When you are all you have left
Johnny Earl has curly hair
Light complexion
Extremely fair
In a scheme of how he will fulfill his dream
With such little money
It seems

Many times, we forget

Importance slips

As we worry about other lives

Our life is ripped

CRIMINAL INTENT {EDIFICATION}

Erotic, Exotic, Hypnotic, Provocative

Is the way I live

In a house high upon a hill

People wonder who I am

Am I a scam

How could I be

When I live in a no man land

Majestic Majesty is the radiance of my being

In world where no one can deceive me

Living accordingly to surroundings I am in

Never having to beg any man

Sexy, extravagant, flamboyant

Is the words

About my cloths and shoes

Not understanding why

When I individualize

The stance of woman could be a stance a queen

Even when life is not as it seems

Make believing she can fulfill her dream

Voluptuous, Figurine, Gorgeous

Says a man

That describes every woman the same

Lacking any preference

Believes he is ahead of the game

Another will claim the fame

In a City saying they have no reason to be ashamed

Majestic Majesty is the radiance of my being

Can you deceive me

With the telephone wireless world

The back of a girl

That knows everything and anyone whom wish they where the only one

In a plot of dismemberment

Not of a limb

Leaving a head and the effervescent of an existence

<u>THEY KNEW</u>

Boar her

Adore her

In a dominant ring

Show her what obsession means

The city lights are high

As I drive by

Late at night

Wondering why

The hand was in a fist

It went in like this

As I went to sleep

How many times do we do what is similar

Trying to become familiar

Lies are the same

In this game

James is what they say utilize

Whom to despise as well as epitomize

Making what they believe is something

Into nothing

Give him what

An ego trip

Why the white woman stole my slip

Dana, Dana, Dana

Why are you between my legs

In a room with a hotel bed

You the cigarette

As well as the shit

As you open your legs

For that black man dick

Boar her

Adore her

Shouts from a far

As I pass by

In my car

<u>ANYWAY I CAN GET IT</u>

Magic is in the hat
Escapes a bat
In a hunted house
Full of cats

Uncle Paul died this past Sunday
Leaving all his children some money
But when the will was read
Only money they found was his paid bail

Past lives are present
Your mother I see
Hanging out clothes that are not clean
As she deploys a plan
On how to change you into a man
While she hunts for Peter Pan

Wicked is the death of your Uncle
In mourning of what could have been
Thorough formulation of a potential win

Why do you think the past is accurate
As you take the same blood through
Is it the face that you feel will hold the power

As I contain laughter hour after hour

Again, why is the glass in your mouth

Licking my ass is not a chose

Keeping your dick in placed is what's voiced

MEDDLE WHO—BE YOU

I am so sorry that you want white ass

I do not know how to began to laugh

Scholarly usually comes more in white

Edification is not really there

Superiority is what is feared

Maiah Cary stands in an environmental force

As if she has no chose

You hear the din dong of the ring bell

This is what this woman calls hell

Misery is in her concept

As she laughs with horse hair

Chiropracticing hysteria

Of what she calls her chose

As I raise my hand to rejoice

The bitch is used and not by force

Open sesame is the white girl legs

As she takes head by head

The man dick cum

As this white bitch pants for some

In essence, would she have a bum

Laugh when something is really funny

You are, but I am not paid enough money

I look at the video without remorse

A white woman really thinking she has a voice

Jealousy has been taken

By a native

Whom do not give a damn

A white man ploy to scam

As he began to exploit his white bitch without shame

Accurate as the finger go in the ass

The back to the split

This is what one would call bullshit

<u>SHOWBIZ</u>

I listen to a rapper call Busta Rhymes

Whom says, "Give It To Me" all the time

He stands in lint at my door

As if he is standing on Mount Rushmore

Entertainment is the circle where you should remain

That is where you can receive proper fame

As I try not to call you a bad name

Love me for what

I do not know

As you talk with a load in your mouth

Doing the bay window in the front of my apartment

Again, are you retarded

Tell me please, over and over again

This will help me win

As I listen to the spring

In the bull pin

Terrorism is what they think they got

When they do not even have ammunition left

"Who want her" is constantly asked

By big dick fagots that are stuck on them self

As they believe they are in my head

Jump out your UKON, wishing me dead

I am sorry you cannot handle it

You have been mislead, placed in bullshit

I am the difference and not the bread

Whom is in whom head

I be damn if I'm scared

<u>INSINUATE</u>

Tight mouth
Touch me
Chewing hard
Rush me
Stomp your feet
Nothing but noise
Fighting should not come so hard

Assimilation of a threat
That can be instigated
By man of all races
Only done toward one person that is hated

Volatile I am not
A scenario of a plot
By people whom forgot
What life is all about

Frowning with a twisted mouth
Rush me
Protruding eyes
Touch me
Screaming at the top of your voice
Nothing but racquet
What are you lacking

Violent nature is not diabolical

Only what you can recall

A potential victim of a quarrel

As you walk into the house

Justification has just be written

With presence that can never be comprehended

In darkness to man

The body begins to spin

"The darkest thing could be the ideology of life itself." (Verlena Sexton-Walker)

CINGULAR WIRELESS

Still the cell phone, right

I be glad when you take my life

Do you ever think twice

That will help you get things right

The presence of body bobs down on the bed

The click of the krinklers by my head

Is the pop of a top on a pop bottle

Raising from the dead

In a possessed bed

Believe me, I am not scared

A sequence of poetry of what is wrong

Never really got it going on

Nothing but fools constantly playing a game

This how the white man looks at fame

"Taking something so easily is the reality of what really is yours to take."
(Verlena Sexton-Walker)

<u>INAPPROPRIATE</u>

Away out yonder

Stays a man in a ponder

Hoping that his ideal will come across

Not all is yet lost

Clinking of the feet

For the eyes to see

And the hope that somebody will tell me

As they deploy a zone

That says, "All is not well"

The family is dollared over and over again

Creating a lost, that can never win

As the back goes against the front

This damn fool is the certain bunt

Clinking of the heals

For the eyes to feel

As a zone is deployed

At your will

Enemies constantly under attack

Is this for real or just an act

The cigarette pats the pack

As the man ask, "Do you know where you are at"

Clinking, Clinking
One, Two times
Clinking, Clinking
From behind
What process is being done
This man says he has truly won
Picking up the telephone

"In a zone, know what you are zoning and why." (Verlena Sexton-Walker)

<u>OBSESSION</u>

Police in the turning lane

Looking at me as if he is insane

Needs his dick suck

By his man

That cannot give him what a woman can

Don't do me because you don't know how

In the mainframe of your database

As you wish my pussy was in your face

The look makes you a disgrace

Why do I constantly smell pist

Is because your dick is in your fist

The psychotic look becomes you

This will help you get through

Write a poem, that's what you need to do

The back against the car tire

As the repairman pumps air

Knowledge in a thought that this is a relationship made

Glorify me each and every day

That you are so easy to persuade

Do not try to be me because you do not know how

Is this body waste part of the car

Making a women believe she has it down pact

This is not a mental attack

But away of life, as a matter-of-fact

"Everything you do is sometimes not for you. Don't be so easily fooled."
(Verlena Sexton-Walker)

<u>PERSONALITY DISCREPANCY</u>

You can't accept rejection and the truth

That is what is wrong with you

Sucking dicks and anal sex is call blue

Maybe that is what you need to do

Waiting on me to apologize

You will keep your mouth filled with flies

That is the technology given to you

Go ahead, remain a damn fool

How small does it has to get for you to leave it along

Disappear, the twilight zone

Never fucking for real

Come on, lie to yourself

That is how you deal

The camole makes a constant sound

Water in the ground

As a nose turns with a frown

This is a face of a clown

Ass is shouted in the wall

Walking away down the hall

Can you now accept rejection, which is the truth

You do not want to be use

Are you that easily confused

OKAY! OKAY!!

Your degree is from a school

"In war of wills, defend yourself first and others last." (Verlena Sexton-Walker)

<u>REPLICA</u>

Words are utilized
When not in disguised
Badness of a child
Who never smiles

Let her
Let her do what
Anything she wants
Let her taunt

Vocabulary is large
This is call smart
By a group of retards

Let her
Let her call
Anytime she wants
Let her front
Language of a man
That says he can
When he spins
He's depicting a win

Let her

Let her fool you

That you are bad

Itching to whip her ass

Conversation is done

None has won

As I walk away

From a bum

Let her is said

Behind my head

As they believe, they can confiscate a bed

"The biggest idiots are those who know what they are doing but can not associate it to common sense." (Verlena Sexton-Walker)

EXCERTION

Tide in the ocean

Tide in the sea

Tide in the river

Are you tired of me

This is the word

That is constantly scream

As they believe, sex is in a dream

Tidal wave

Tidal pool

Tidal being tired of you

This is the presumption of a fool

Whom forgot to finish school

Surfing the tide

Riding the tide

Tired of the tide

The enjoyment is finally finish

What can be done within a minute

"Words that can be confused, usually does not cause confusion." (Verlena Sexton-Walker)

50 CENTS STYLE

I'm not a gangster

I'm not a thug

I'm not your paradise

If you meet me, you'll discover, I'm not that very nice

The police call me Criminal Insane

To keep me in pain

When all they are giving me is unknown fame

The ghetto is not where I am from

I know nothing about living in slubs

In life, I can relate to a bum

When with my man, I am the only one

The love doctor call me Casanova

Never having to wish on a four-leaf clover

Moving to the next man, because this relationship is over

I am not a gangster

I am not a thug

I am not your paradise

If you meet me, you will discover, I am not that very nice

The police call me Criminal Insane

To keep me in pain

When all they are giving me is unknown fame

The love doctor call me Casanova

Never having to wish on a four-leaf clover

Moving to the next man, because this relationship is over

The police and love doctor are not the only ones

That wish they could get some

When porno graphing says ejaculate so I can cum

Again, the ghetto is not where I am from

I know nothing about living in slubs

In life, I can depict a bum

When with my man, I am the only one

"Remember sex is only good to those whom do not have it." (Verlena Sexton-Walker)

<u>CLINICAL SOCIAL WORKER</u>

Early in the morning

Shit in the corner

Detroit Bitch don't clean her house

And you wonder why

She says she does not wanna

So I confront her

Saying, "Look at all those blow flies"

Bitch, your nasty ass should die

Babies in the kitchen

Did I forget to mention

Eating a pudding pie

Blow flies swarms her

Not really harming her

But, puts a star on her eye

And you wonder why

Unsanitary plus binary

Brings tears to your eyes

Double the trouble

The laughter transpires

The nasty Detroit bitch should be despise

And you wonder why

Shit in the corner

She talks to me with a too much persona
Letting me know what she is all about
Impression is in place
She asks, "Why should I be disgrace?"
As laughter went in her face
My response, "You have won"
Shaking my head knowing where she was placed

You wonder why

Shit in the corner
Early in the morning
Detroit bitch children waste

"My effervescent, my sheer existence - that makes me better than you - tells me I have more work to do" (Verlena Sexton-Walker)

UNCUT UNCENSORED/UNCENSORED UNCUT

All of me belong to me

None of me belongs to he/she

Uplift my dignity

By trying to disgrace me

I am the foreseer of destiny

An outcome is in my grasp

Embarrass me, I think not

All of me is me

None of me is he/she

Overcoming jealousies

That is prevalent in my life

I do not have to strife or fight

I foresee the destiny

Amazing in the making

Without sacrifice

All of me belong to me

None me is he/she

Never am I mislead

Always ahead

As I discover, whom wish me dead

Or rather wish they where sleeping in my bed

"Stay family orient, all I said, I meant it"—VSW—VERLENA SEXTON-WALKER

FOR WHOM SO DESIRE…{LIFE STRUGGLES DIALOGUE}

As I attempt to bend my knees

A prayer is received

Of all the things I can achieve

In the mist of victory

I open my hand to the lifeline

That reads mankind

In this palm of mine

Attempting to bend my knees

Praying is perceived

Things I must achieve

Am I in the mist of victory

This is what I pray…

God as people surround to cause me harm

Send your forgotten son

So that they will know I am not the one to be shun

Nor am I Jesus Christ

The one whom was crucified

Not even a sacrifice

A question God, "In this life do 'we' ever think twice?"

Amazing is the disgrace when all is in the mist a grace. Is this what we call 'Agrape?' - VSW -

Loving one[self] is truly guidance to success. This is the only help. -VSW-

LIFE STRUGGLES DIALOGUED...

<u>GIST</u>

Young roam

Old home

Name game

Always lame

Quest for fame

Man wipe

Card swipe

Money spent

Richness sent

What is meant

Open palm

Reward some

Magnify a bum

Not the one

Standing tall

Bald head and all

Defending whom

Who has room

Never to soon

<u>POETIC CHILD VERSES</u>

The sky

The sun

The moon

Have fun

Raining outside

Quietness of a child

Mankind stands and smile

The air

The heat

A popping sheet

Friends embrace as they meet

Mud slouching my shoes

As I play while in school

With whom I chose

Children poetry in a rhythm

As laughter makes the eyes shines

<u>MISSIONARY STATEMENT</u>

Interaction

Communication

Hesitation

Procrastination

You cannot make me relate

Psychology is your mistake

M.J. family counselor

Looks at food on my table

Tells me his mind is disable

V.C. and the picture tube

Television man still in school

Subject to being mentally used

A.I. through the white man

That hangs my ceiling fans

On bended knees says, "You are Verlena Sexton"

Response, "You are in destination"

J.S. and Von

Designating himself as the one

To be depicted through a bum

K.G. pushed from behind

In a bathroom, that is mine

Saying, "We will really do her next time"

M.M. always yelling hair

Coming out the carpet unbare

To do the head is his plan

This is a damn fool call a man

Ms. Littlejon is in my hall

V.C. says this is his call

As he believes, I told him all

Watch Mighty Joe Young fall

Remember, this is Verlena call

"If everyone knew their calling whom would do all the work?" (Verlena Sexton-Walker)

<u>CREATIVITY</u>

Let us began this conversation through meditation

Of mind, body, and soul

As our lifelines, unfold

My name is Verlena Sexton with the Walker still attached

I am a psychotherapist, as a matter-of-fact

Divorce for three years

From a husband of the Black race

Who could not keep the pace

Marriage again

Is very slim

A diabolical win

Next,

My name is Gracie Jones

I have to guard my tone

This is what I am told

As I unfold

I am a mediator

I married a year ago

Any cheers to hear before I go

Last,

My name is Marvin Tools

I drive a Greyhound Bus

So many people travel

Keeping up fuss

There are ten people in the room

Any more volunteers

All remaining shake their heads (no)

As they drink beers

{(As a writing test, add on your version [as you see them] of the other seven)}

ABOUT THE AUTHOR

Verlena Sexton-Walker is an amazing author of poetry whom poetry exemplifies wrongs in life that surpasses crime and chooses. She is a Native American born in raised in the Mississippi Delta in which she also possesses the gift of spiritual healer. This is Verlena second book of poetry and as always, much enjoyment to the reader lies within the pages.